TO GIVE YOU A FUTURE WITH HOPE

OTHER BOOKS BY DAVID HAAS AVAILABLE
FROM GIA PUBLICATIONS, INC.

With Every Note I Sing (G-4392)

I Will Sing Forever (G-5649)

A Time to Pray: With the Old Testament (G-6722)

A Time to Pray: With the New Testament (G-6654)

A Time to Pray: For Justice and Peace (G-6868)

To Worship in Spirit and Truth: A Liturgical Preparation Process
for Pastoral Musicians and Liturgical Leaders (G-6521)

Biblical Way of the Cross (G-6615)

The Holy Presence of God: Daily Prayer for Youth, Teachers, Catechists,
and Youth Ministers (G-7154)

For additional printed music, recordings, and resources by David Haas
available from GIA Publications, Inc., please visit www.giamusic.com.

G-7153

DAVID HAAS
TO GIVE YOU A FUTURE WITH HOPE

Prayers, Blessings, Meditations, and Challenges
for young people and all who walk with them

GIA Publications, Inc.
Chicago

Art direction and design by Kantor Group, Inc., Minneapolis, MN, www.kantorgroup.com
Edited by Helen Haas and Tom Backen

Scripture quotations, unless otherwise noted, are from the New Revised Standard Version of the Bible, Copyright © 1989 by the Division of Christian Education of the National Council of the Churches of Christ in the U.S.A.

All quotations from the Book of Psalms, unless otherwise noted, are from the Grail, Copyright © 1963, 1986, 1993, 2000 The Grail. All rights reserved.
Published through exclusive license agreement by GIA Publications, Inc.

Copyright © 2007 GIA Publications, Inc
7404 South Mason Avenue
Chicago, Illinois 60638
International Copyright Secured.
All Rights Reserved.

Printed in the United States of America

G-7153
ISBN: 978-1-57999-677-2

For Tom Backen —

master teacher, servant guide, caring mentor,
committed advocate, tireless seeker,
movie lover, pie maker, gentle spirit, tender heart,
friendship builder, faithful colleague,
wisdom presence

with gratitude

For surely I know the plans I have for you,
says the Lord,
plans for your welfare and not for harm,
to give you a future with hope.

Jeremiah 29:11

TABLE OF CONTENTS

Preface ix
In Gratitude xiii
Introduction: Praying Is Not Easy by Bill Huebsch xvii

Morning Prayers 1
Evening and Night Prayers 9
Traditional and Common Prayers 19
Prayers for the Liturgical Seasons 25
    Advent 25
    Christmas Season 28
    Lent 30
    Holy Week 33
    Easter Season 34
Prayers, Meditations, and Touchstones from Scripture 37
Prayers, Meditations, and Challenges from the Wisdom Community . . . 49
Prayers for Various Occasions and Circumstances 63
Prayers and Meditations for Peace, Compassion, and Justice 75
Meal Blessings 85
More Prayers and Blessings 89

References 95
About the Author 99

PREFACE

To Give You a Future with Hope is a collection of prayers, blessings, meditations, touchstones, and challenges for use in a wide variety of settings—in the classroom or chapel, at prayer services, formation events, retreats, or at any other event where young people gather to grow in faith—either alone or with adult leaders such as teachers, youth and campus ministers, parents, catechists, and pastors. These texts can be read or prayed alone quietly, or read with others in small or large groups. This resource can be used alone or with its companion volume, *The Holy Presence of God*.

As the author of this collection, I too struggle with prayer, and I am always looking for the profound word, phrase, or poetic turn that will move the heart toward a perfect communion with God. All of us get distracted far too often and make excuses not to take the time to pray. We often feel emptiness or develop a certain cynicism when our prayers do not seem to be listened to or result in an answer we do not like.

But, in the midst of it all, praying is critical for believers. To be a Christian means to pray to a God who is beyond our understanding. To engage in a conversation with God is the noblest and highest articulation of discipleship in which we can take part. To follow in the path of God means that we must praise, give thanks, present our sorrow, cry out in need, listen well, and do so with other pilgrims who possess the same ache we do. When we take this step and agree to wrestle with God in prayer, we then remember that God truly does answer prayer even if we do not always like or agree with the answer.

Prayer needs to be an honest journey, one accompanied by a sense of humility, to understand that God is who God is and we are who we are. Any prayer text, however poetic or mundane in its aesthetic presentation, always surrenders to the fact that prayer is not about us telling God what we want; rather, its purpose is to call us to listen to what God is trying so desperately to say to us.

This collection aims to help all of us—young and old—in this journey of prayer. These prayers are arranged in separate sections, some according to the time of day, others from the tradition, the liturgical year or Scripture; some were written for a number of different settings or circumstances that require a prayer or text to help focus the occasion. Many of the prayers here are new original texts alongside prayers and meditations drawn from other sources, both traditional and contemporary. Great saints and spiritual giants as well as relatively unknown authors composed the prayers. All express genuine yearnings of the human heart, reaching toward a power beyond our understanding. To invite those in our care to the wonder and mysteries of prayer is one of the greatest callings we have as believing Christians.

The sections in this book are arranged according to the following themes and areas of focus.

MORNING PRAYERS

This first section contains prayers, blessings, and other meditations to begin the day. Included is an abbreviated service for morning adapted from the official prayer of the Church: the Liturgy of the Hours.

EVENING AND NIGHT PRAYERS

Similar to the previous section, included here are several prayerful texts for evening (traditionally seen as the time of sunset), and nighttime (just before going to sleep). Also included is an abbreviated evening prayer service.

TRADITIONAL AND COMMON PRAYERS

This section includes many well-known and beloved prayers from the tradition.

PRAYERS FOR THE LITURGICAL SEASONS

These are new weekly prayers for use during the seasons of the liturgical year, specifically Advent, Christmas, Lent, Holy Week, and Easter.

PRAYERS, MEDITATIONS, AND TOUCHSTONES FROM SCRIPTURE

Included in this section are powerful offerings from both the Hebrew Scriptures (Old Testament) and the Christian New Testament. In particular, many verses from the psalms are included here, speaking to the many different seasons of the human condition and particularly appropriate to the spiritual journey of young people.

PRAYERS, MEDITATIONS, AND CHALLENGES FROM THE WISDOM COMMUNITY
These texts carry the wisdom of many of the Christian saints and many other holy women and men throughout history. They provide rich insight and depth of spirit for young and old alike.

PRAYERS FOR VARIOUS OCCASIONS AND CIRCUMSTANCES
The several prayers in this chapter are specifically designed to help speak to specific circumstances and situations for young people, teachers, and other leaders.

PRAYERS AND MEDITATIONS FOR PEACE, COMPASSION, AND JUSTICE
In this section we find many profound words of wisdom that echo the central themes of Catholic social teaching, a critical thread in the formation of young people.

MEAL BLESSINGS
Included are well-known and not-so-familiar blessings and prayers for gathering at table.

MORE PRAYERS AND BLESSINGS
The final section includes additional prayers and blessings that can enrich any gathering of young people and adults—alone or together.

It is important to remember that when it comes to prayer, what is of ultimate importance is not how or what one prays, but that we pray—period. Fundamentally, prayer is not something we study or talk about; rather, it is something that we, as believers, do, regardless of our age or where we might be on the journey.

Enjoy and revel in the prayers and offerings of wisdom found in these pages. May they become touchstones to deepen our ongoing faith conversation with God and to help our young people move into a future with hope.

—David Haas

IN GRATITUDE

With this book and its complementary volume, *The Holy Presence of God,* it is important to give thanks to God for the many who have accompanied me on the journey in developing these resources and who have always been such good and supportive friends. I first want to give thanks to Alec Harris and everyone at GIA Publications for being a source of patience and support in my ministerial activities. I want to offer special thanks to Elizabeth Dallman Bentley for her editorial assistance, and also to Kelly Dobbs Mickus, Michael Cymbala, Bob Batastini, Tom Hawley, Suzanne Orland, and Cathy Kennerk for always being so supportive. I am so thankful to my friend and "scripture-mentor" Art Zannoni for continually opening up for me the profound beauty of the Bible and uncovering how the Psalms are a central cornerstone of prayer for Jews and Christians alike. I also want to thank Fr. Michael Joncas for his faithful friendship and for all that I have learned from him about theology, ministry, liturgy, prayer, and the sacramental life and for his love of the Liturgy of the Hours, which continues to be an important center of my own spiritual life.

I am very thankful to Lori True for her creativity, her passion, her commitment to quality prayer, her friendship, and the endless well of ideas and challenge that she always brings to the table. I also want to thank Lori together with my colleague and fellow theology teacher Joel Loecken and my friend and hero Sr. Helen Prejean, CSJ, for continually awakening in me the importance of prayer's partnership with social justice and Catholic social teaching. I will always be grateful to my friend Kate Cuddy for her witness and care in her work with young people, who, together with Jim Hamburge, invited me years ago to enter into the Catholic high school experience—what a ride! I am also grateful to Leisa Anslinger for her friendship, her ongoing encouragement, and her commitment to prayer serving lifelong catechesis and formation.

God bless my friend Bill Huebsch for writing the wonderful introduction to this book and for his gift of weaving words with theology. His approach has significantly influenced how I approach the fragile craft of designing texts for communal prayer. I am grateful to my dear friend Tom Franzak for his friendship and humor and for helping me to appreciate the lives and spirituality of the saints and how their lives of prayer serve the spiritual search of believers. Love and thanks go to Fr. Ray East for living the joy of his faith, which is at the center of any life of prayer, and to my friends Fr. George DeCosta, Joe Camacho, Fr. Alapaki Kim, Tony Alonso, Peter Kolar, and Fr. Ricky Manalo, CSP, for their ministry blending the life of prayer with cultural identity and tradition. Thanks to Sr. Roberta Kolasa, SJ, and Sr. Gertrude Foley, SC, for being such wonderful mentors and witnesses of faith and ministry, and to Jo Infante, whose entire life has been a prayerful inspiration in my life. I want to express my gratitude to Fr. Richard Rohr, OFM, Megan McKenna, Marcus Borg, Walter Brueggemann, Jim Wallis, Bart Ehrman, Diana Hayes, Sr. Joan Chittister, OSB, and to the loving memory of Henri Nouwen, Madelin Sue Martin, Archbishop Oscar Romero, Dorothy Day, Ralph Kiefer, Bishop Kenneth Untener, Leon Roberts, Derek Campbell, and Fr. Jim Dunning. Their writings, theology, vision, witness, and prayerful lives have sustained me in my hope and passion for ministry and the faith.

I want to also offer my thanks to friends John Roberto, Sr. Bridget Waldorf, SSND, Jesse Manibusan, Sr. Edith Prendergast, RC, Michael Carotta, Fr. Joe Kempf, Tom East, and Anna Scally for their ministerial wisdom and work in youth ministry and catechesis and to Sr. Kathleen Storms, SSND, for how she has made the spiritual walk with me for many years and helped me to integrate my life of prayer with the joys, blessings, aches, and pains of life and ministry. My love goes out to Rob and Mary Glover and their family, Mary Werner, Bonnie Faber, Michael Griffin, Dan Kantor, Rob Strusinski, Barbara Conley-Waldmiller, Marty Haugen, Lisa Biedenbach, Carol Porter, Stephen Petrunak, Steve Kron, Matt Reichert, Sr. Andrea Lee, IHM, Tim Westerhaus, Jim Waldo, Br. Dennis Schmitz, MM, Kathy and Glen Baybayan, David Dreher, and Eileen Bird for their tremendous friendship. I also want to send my thanks to Fr. Michael Byron and the praying community of St. Cecilia's in St. Paul, Minnesota; to the Music Ministry Alive! family. And to Mom, Dad, Colleen, Jeffrey, and Helen for their unconditional love and support.

Lastly, I want to make known my thanks to Dr. Bob Tift and the Benilde-St. Margaret's School community in St. Louis Park, Minnesota, especially Mary Periolat, Maura Brew, Mary Kay

Werner, Tom Backen, Mary Glover, Sr. Jeanne Marie Vanderlinde, OSB, Joel Loecken, Becca Walsh, Sue Cipolle, Janet Scheinost, May Lane, Holly Hoey-Germann, Nancy Stockhaus, Paul Keefe, Connie Fourre, and Mick Hawkins for the wonderful well of support and friendship that they give. I am grateful for the experience in serving this community; my life and time with them have served as the genesis for these resources of prayer, and for that I am so grateful.

Soli Deo Gloria!

—David Haas

INTRODUCTION

PRAYING IS NOT EASY

I'll bet you're like most young people. For you, learning to pray is not easy. Prayer demands a relationship with God and others in which you allow God to enter into you in ways that are unexpected and often surprising. It touches the very center of your person. Here, where you are alone with God, you hear a voice speaking in the midst of your busy life. You must *pause* to allow this to happen. *Pause* and *listen*.

And as you well know, even as a student or young worker, pausing like this takes *time*.

Time. It's the thing we don't have, isn't it? I mean, the radio is playing. The Internet is humming. The TV is on. One of our several phones is ringing. We have appointments to keep, demands to be met, and schedules to follow. But, even in the din of such a busy life, the Divine One speaks in your heart. You are touched and healed. You are made more whole and more real. What comes to light then—matters you might prefer to leave in the darkness are included in this—has the power to change your life forever.

In this wonderful book, David Haas provides you with a pathway for such powerful prayer. *To Give You a Future with Hope* steps into your busy life as a student or young worker: school, jobs, friends, family, parish, band, sports, theater, more friends, the slow dawning of adulthood with all its aches and pains. . . . It steps into that with you and provides you with a friend and mentor who can help guide you to pray well.

We tend to resist prayer. With the same force with which we grip our cell phones or Blackberries, we hold on for dear life to the fast-moving busy-ness of our lives because if we can just keep busy, then the pain of loneliness, or rejection, or self-dislike, or apparent failure can all be kept at a distance. We tend to hope in things that bring us no comfort, or perhaps sometimes *we do not have hope in the future at all*. But if you could just let go for a moment and let God enter into all of that with you, you will find strength, hope, acceptance, and love. That's why David Haas wrote *To Give You a Future with Hope*. He's offering you that hope once again.

So pick up this book often. Carry it with you. Read and know these prayers. Memorize some of them. Let these prayers touch your heart and move it in the direction of the Divine One who loves you and waits for you.

If you haven't been praying for a while, be aware that your first prayer may be a little painful. You will feel like you're giving up time for it, and if you really allow yourself to be present to the powerful, ever-present God, your heart will be touched in ways you don't expect. That can be painful at first. But once you discover prayer you will never want to let it go. You will never want to stop. Whenever there is silence around you, in the night as you try to sleep, your mind will turn to God, and you will offer yourself to God, expecting only love in return.

Now, here's a word to those of you reading this who are not students or young workers. *To Give You a Future with Hope* is also a great resource for you! It's a resource for all of us. Indeed, we all live busy lives these days, and often we put our hopes in that which produces only more anxiety and even despair. Let this powerful book help you with daily prayer because, for all of us, learning to pray is not easy!

—Bill Huebsch
Pine City, Minnesota

MORNING PRAYERS

GOOD MORNING

God,
good morning.

Come and fill our day with new breath
so that we may become a living hymn of praise to you.

As we begin this day,
we thank you that last night
was not our last night.

For one more day,
you have given us the gift of life.
May we embrace all that you are to us,
the light from heaven and songs of the earth,
the joy of our hearts,
and the hope of all our dreaming.

This day, may your love be our calling,
and may we proclaim your power and promise.

A new day.
A new encounter with you.
A new reason to sing.

For this, we give you thanks.

Amen.

— *DH*

HEAR, O ISRAEL

Hear, O Israel: The Eternal is our God,
The Eternal God is One.
Let us praise God who rules in glory forever and ever.
You shall love the Lord your God,
with all your heart,
and with all your soul,
and with all your might.
Keep these words that I am commanding you today
in your heart.
Recite them to your children and talk about them
when you are at home and when you are away,
when you lie down and when you rise.
Bind them as a sign on your hand,
fix them as an emblem on your forehead,
and write them on the doorposts of your house and on your gates.

— SHEMA / *Deuteronomy 6:4–9*

PRAYER FOR THE MORNING

God,
we greet this day and you
with joy and thanks.

Over and over again, you give us another day,
another gift, another adventure.

We greet you with all that we have,
with all that we are, with all our heart,
filled with thanks for bringing us
through the darkness of night once again.

We commit ourselves
to keeping you at the center of our day.
Our thoughts, our actions,
our words, and our gifts—
they are for you.

Come and fill us with your presence,
so that with every breath,
every utterance, every gesture,
and every glance,
we may see you in all things.

Thank you for another day.

Amen.

— *DH*

WAKE ME UP

God, wake me up this morning,
even if I might not like it.

— *Jim Cotter*

HELP ME REMEMBER

Lord, help me to remember
that nothing is going to happen today
that you and I cannot handle together.

— *Saidie Patterson*

A BRIEF MORNING PRAYER SERVICE

OPENING

As the opening dialogue begins, all make the sign of the cross.

LEADER: God, come to my assistance.

ALL: **Lord, make haste to help me.**

LEADER: Glory be to the Father,
and to the Son,
and to the Holy Spirit;

ALL: **As it was in the beginning,
is now,
and will be forever. Amen.**

THE PRAYING OF THE PSALMS

The praying of one or more psalms is part of the rich tradition of morning prayer. Psalm 63 is considered to be the traditional psalm for morning prayer. Some other psalms that are appropriate for morning prayer include Psalms 8, 95, and 100.

PSALM 63 (ADAPTED)

LEADER: As morning breaks, I look to you to be my strength.

ALL: **As morning breaks, I look to you to be my strength.**

LEADER: You are my God whom I long for,
for you my soul is thirsting.
Like a dry and waterless land,
my soul thirsts and aches for you.

ALL: **As morning breaks, I look to you to be my strength.**

LEADER: I look and mediate upon you in your holy place,
to see your power and your glory.
Your love, O God, is better than life itself,
and my mouth will sing praise to you.

ALL: **As morning breaks, I look to you to be my strength.**

LEADER: I will bless you always, each and every day,
and in your name I will raise my hands in prayer.
My soul will feast like the richness of a banquet,
and I will praise you with joy.

ALL: **As morning breaks, I look to you to be my strength.**

LEADER: As I lie in bed, I remember you,
and I think about you all night long.
You have always been there to help me,
and in the shadow of your wings I shout for joy.
I cling to you, and you keep me safe.

ALL: **As morning breaks, I look to you to be my strength.**

A time for silent prayer follows.

READING FROM SCRIPTURE

At this point, someone reads a passage from Scripture appropriate for the day or time of year.

A period of silence should follow for meditation on the Word of God.

GOSPEL CANTICLE (ADAPTED FROM LUKE 1:68–79)

After hearing from the Word of God, Christians have traditionally responded by praying or singing together the Canticle of Zachary, a song of praise that comes from the Gospel of Luke.

ALL: **Blest are you, O God our Savior,
you have come to set us free.**

 **You raise up a child of power
from the house of David, your own;
you have promised freedom from evil,
as stories told from long ago.**

 **Mercy is your promise to us,
always true, remembered by all;
we are free from fear to worship
for all our days.**

 **You, O child, are a gift to your people,
you go forth to show us the way,
singing the good news of salvation
through the forgiveness of our sins.**

 **Your bright morning is our compassion,
breaking through the darkness of night;
shining on those beneath the shadows,
guiding our feet to ways of peace.**

 **Blest are you, O God our Savior,
for you have come to set us free.**

INTERCESSIONS / THE LORD'S PRAYER

The sample prayers provided here can be followed by specific prayers of concern offered by those coming together.

LEADER: For all leaders, for strength
 as they make decisions for the good of all, we pray:

ALL: **Lord, come and bless your people.**

LEADER: For all who suffer from the despair of hunger,
war, abuse, violence, loneliness, and hatred, we pray:

ALL: **Lord, come and bless your people.**

LEADER: For all who have died, we pray:

ALL: **Lord, come and bless your people.**

LEADER: For all of us gathered together now,
for hope in the midst of our needs and concerns,
we pray:

ALL: **Lord, come and bless your people.**

LEADER: For peace in our world, our country,
our community, our families, and our hearts, we pray:

ALL: **Lord, come and bless your people.**

At this time, those gathered can take a moment to add their own prayers.

LEADER: For all these prayers,
and for those in the quiet of our hearts, we pray:

ALL: **Lord, come and bless your people.**

LEADER: Gathering all of our prayers and praise into one,
let us now pray with the prayer that Christ himself gave
to us:

ALL: **Our Father . . .**

FINAL PRAYER
LEADER: Gracious and awesome God,
We know that you are with us,
and we believe you listen and walk with us
throughout our day.

Be with us today
as we seek to be your sons and daughters,
your people.

We ask this through Christ our Lord.

ALL: **Amen.**

BLESSING / SIGN OF PEACE
All then pray a blessing for each other.

ALL: **May God bless and keep us;
may God smile on us.
May God show us kindness
and fill us with peace.
May God bless us,
Father, Son, and Spirit.
May we always love and serve,
filled with God's peace.**

The prayer concludes with the sharing of the sign of peace.

EVENING AND NIGHT PRAYERS

A PRAYER FOR THE EVENING

God,
you have walked with us all day,
and for this we thank you.

Once again, you have loved us enough
to bring us to the end of this day safe
and secure in your presence.

It is our prayer and hope
that in all our activities
we gave glory to you.

Thank you for another day.
Help us to greet this evening in your peace.

Amen.

— *DH*

AS THE EVENING BEGINS

God,
as the evening begins,
as the sun sails into the distance,
I thank you with all that I am.

Thank you for this day,
for your loving, your giving,
your faithfulness and presence,
throughout all that has happened and occurred.

It is my hope and my prayer that I kept you close.

As the evening comes, keep my focus on you.
As the evening comes, keep my heart pure.
As the evening comes, may I become your peace.

Thank you for today.

Amen.

— DH

A NIGHT PRAYER

God,
Thank you for the mystery of the night,
the home and holder of dreams.
Nourish the upcoming sleep
with stories of the depth of your love.
May the wonderful images that lie ahead
dream a new vision of your love.
Thank you for the gift of stars, the brightness of the moon,
and all the sounds of night.

Help me not to be fearful of the night,
but to embrace it as the center of peace.
May I hold the silence, which is the best music of all,
because it is there where you dwell most clearly
and where you call me most honestly to live in faithfulness to you.

Good night.

Amen.

— DH

IN BEAUTY WE WALK

In beauty we walk;
With beauty before us, we walk.
With beauty behind us, we walk.
With beauty above us, we walk.
With beauty above us and about us, we walk.
It is finished in beauty.

— *a Navajo night chant*

WATCH, O LORD

Watch, O Lord, with all those awake this night,
Watch, O Lord, with all those who weep;
Give your angels and saints charge over all who sleep.

Tend your ailing ones;
Rest your weary ones;
Bless your dying ones:
In your love, O Lord of all.

Soothe your suffering ones;
Heal afflicted ones;
Shield your joyous ones;
In your love, O Lord of all.

Hold your grieving ones;
Raise your fallen ones;
Mend your broken ones;
In your love, O Lord of all.

Guard your little ones;
Guide your searching ones;
Grant us all your peace;
In your love, O Lord of all.

— *Staint Augustine, adapted by Marty Haugen*

WHEN I REST IN GOD

When I rest in God,
the fearful dreams stay away.

— *DH*

HELP ME TO LET GO

God,
as I find myself in the stillness,
help me to let go.

Help me to let go
of all that has happened this day,
good and bad,
all of the activities,
the joy, the anxieties,
the stress,
and all that stirs in me
still at this moment.

As the stars of night surround me,
help me to dream well.
Help me to savor the stories and images
that will visit me this night.

Help me to embrace this night,
and take away my fear.
Help me to partner with the silence
and to discover and listen
to what it may teach me.

You are here with me.
Hold me close,
and help to bring forth the morning once again.

Good night.

Amen.

— *DH*

LET ME SLEEP IN YOUR ARMS

Now that the sun has set,
I sit and rest and think of you.
Give my weary body peace.
Let my legs and arms stop aching.
Let my nose stop sneezing.
Let my head stop thinking.
Let me sleep in your arms.

— *prayer of the Dinka people, Sudan*

A BRIEF EVENING PRAYER SERVICE

OPENING

As the opening dialogue begins, all make the sign of the cross.

LEADER: God, come to my assistance.

ALL: **Lord, make haste to help me.**

LEADER: Glory be to the Father,
and to the Son,
and to the Holy Spirit;

ALL: **As it was in the beginning,
is now,
and will be forever. Amen.**

THE PRAYING OF THE PSALMS

The praying of one or more psalms is part of the rich tradition of evening prayer. Psalm 141 is considered to be the traditional psalm for evening prayer. Some other psalms that are appropriate for evening prayer include Psalms 4, 91, and 121.

PSALM 141 (ADAPTED)

LEADER: My prayers rise before you like incense,
my hands like an evening offering to you.

ALL: **My prayers rise before you like incense,
my hands like an evening offering to you.**

LEADER: Come quickly, O God, I call to you;
listen to my prayer.
May my prayer rise before you like incense;
My hands are raised high,
like an evening sacrifice.

ALL: **My prayers rise before you like incense,
my hands like an evening offering to you.**

LEADER: Set a guard over my mouth;
watch over my thoughts and words;
keep evil from me.
May I never join the wicked at their table.

ALL: **My prayers rise before you like incense,
my hands like an evening offering to you.**

LEADER: The just ones may keep me pure,
for their rebuke is kindness to me.
Let not the wicked anoint my head;
I will pray against their hateful path.

ALL: **My prayers rise before you like incense,
my hands like an evening offering to you.**

LEADER: Lord, my God, I turn to you;
in you I find safety and refuge.
Do not take my life from me.

ALL: My prayers rise before you like incense,
my hands like an evening offering to you.

A time for silent prayer follows.

READING FROM SCRIPTURE
At this point, someone reads a passage from Scripture appropriate for the day or time of year.

A period of silence should follow for meditation on the Word of God.

GOSPEL CANTICLE (ADAPTED FROM LUKE 1:46–55)
After hearing from the Word of God, Christians have traditionally responded by praying or singing together the Canticle of Mary, also called the Magnificat, a song of praise that comes from the Gospel of Luke.

ALL: **All that I am,
sings of the God who brings new life to birth in me.
My spirit soars on the wings of my Lord!**

**My soul gives glory to the Lord,
rejoicing in my saving God;
who looks upon me in my state,
and all the world will call me blest;
for God works marvels in my sight,
and holy, holy is God's name!**

**God's mercy is from age to age,
on those who follow in fear;
whose arm is power and strength
and scatters all the proud of heart;
who casts the mighty from their thrones,
and raises up the lowly ones!**

**God fills the starving with good things,
the rich are left with empty hands;
protecting all the faithful ones,
remembering Israel with mercy;
the promises known to those before,
and to their children forever.**

**All that I am,
sings of the God who brings new life to birth in me.
My spirit soars on the wings of my Lord!**

INTERCESSIONS / THE LORD'S PRAYER

The sample prayers provided here can be followed by specific prayers of concern offered by those coming together.

LEADER: For all who lead and guide the church,
and for all who lead nations and peoples, we pray:

ALL: **Lord, hear our prayer.**

LEADER: For all who suffer from oppression and hatred,
and for the poor, the hungry, the lonely, and the afraid,
we pray:

ALL: **Lord, hear our prayer.**

LEADER: For all who have died, we pray:

ALL: **Lord, hear our prayer.**

LEADER: For all of us gathered together now,
for hope in the midst of our needs and concerns,
we pray:

ALL: **Lord, hear our prayer.**

LEADER: For peace in our world, our country,
our community, our families, and our hearts, we pray:

ALL: **Lord, hear our prayer.**

At this time, those gathered can take some time to add their own prayers.

LEADER: For all these prayers,
and for those in the quiet of our hearts, we pray:

ALL: **Lord, hear our prayer.**

LEADER: Gathering all of our prayers and praise into one,
let us now pray with the prayer that Christ himself gave
to us:

ALL: **Our Father . . .**

FINAL PRAYER

LEADER: Gracious and awesome God,
we thank you for walking with us today.
Keep us safe always
in the mercy and embrace
of your love and care.

We ask this through Christ our Lord.

ALL: **Amen.**

BLESSING / SIGN OF PEACE

All then pray a blessing for each other.

ALL: **May God bless and keep us;**
may God smile on us.
May God show us kindness
and fill us with peace.
May God bless us,
Father, Son, and Spirit.
May we always love and serve,
filled with God's peace.

The prayer concludes with the sharing of the sign of peace.

TRADITIONAL AND COMMON PRAYERS

THE SIGN OF THE CROSS

In the name of the Father,
and of the Son,
and of the Holy Spirit.

Amen.

THE LORD'S PRAYER (TRADITIONAL)

Our Father, who art in heaven,
hallowed be thy name;
thy kingdom come;
thy will be done on earth as it is in heaven.
Give us this day our daily bread;
and forgive us our trespasses
as we forgive those who trespass against us;
and lead us not into temptation,
but deliver us from evil.
For the kingdom, the power,
and the glory are yours,
now and forever.

Amen.

THE LORD'S PRAYER (CONTEMPORARY)

Our Father in heaven,
hallowed be your name,
your kingdom come,
your will be done, on earth as in heaven.
Give us today our daily bread.
Forgive us our sins
as we forgive those who sin against us.
Save us from the time of trial
and deliver us from evil.
For the kingdom, the power,
and the glory are yours,
now and forever.

Amen.

THE DOXOLOGY

Glory be to the Father,
and to the Son, and to the Holy Spirit:
as it was in the beginning, is now,
and will be forever.

Amen.

HAIL MARY

Hail Mary, full of grace,
the Lord is with you.
Blessed are you among women,
and blessed is the fruit or your womb, Jesus.
Holy Mary, Mother of God,
pray for us sinners
now and at the hour of our death.

Amen.

THE APOSTLES' CREED

We believe in God, the Father almighty,
creator of heaven and earth.

We believe in Jesus Christ, his only Son, our Lord.
He was conceived by the power of the Holy Spirit
and born of the Virgin Mary.
He suffered under Pontius Pilate,
was crucified, died, and was buried.
He descended to the dead.
On the third day he arose again.
He ascended into heaven,
and is seated at the right hand of the Father.
He will come again to judge the living and the dead.

We believe in the Holy Spirit,
the holy catholic Church,
the communion of saints,
the forgiveness of sins,
the resurrection of the body,
and the life everlasting.

Amen.

COME, HOLY SPIRIT

Come, Holy Spirit,
fill the hearts of your faithful
and enkindle in them the fire of your love.

V. Send forth your Spirit, and they shall be created.
R. And you shall renew the face of the earth.

STATIONS OF THE CROSS (TRADITIONAL)

We adore you, O Christ, and we bless you;
because by your holy cross you have redeemed the world.

1. Jesus is condemned to death.
2. Jesus bears his cross.
3. Jesus falls the first time.
4. Jesus meets his mother.

5. Jesus is helped by Simon of Cyrene.
6. Veronica wipes the face of Jesus.
7. Jesus falls a second time.
8. Jesus meets the weeping women.
9. Jesus falls a third time.
10. Jesus is stripped of his garments.
11. Jesus is crucified.
12. Jesus dies.
13. Jesus is taken down from the cross.
14. Jesus is placed in the tomb.

BIBLICAL STATIONS OF THE CROSS
(FROM POPE JOHN PAUL II)

1. Jesus prays in the Garden of Olives. (Luke 22:39–46)
2. Jesus is betrayed by Judas. (Matthew 26:45–49)
3. Jesus is condemned to death by the Sanhedrin. (Mark 14:56, 61–64)
4. Jesus is denied by Peter. (Luke 22:54–62)
5. Jesus is judged by Pilate. (Luke 23:20–25)
6. Jesus is scourged and crowned with thorns. (John 19:1–3)
7. Jesus carries his cross. (John 19:17)
8. Jesus is helped by Simon of Cyrene. (Mark 15:20–21)
9. Jesus encounters the women of Jerusalem. (Luke 23:27–31)
10. Jesus is crucified. (Mark 15:22–26)
11. Jesus promises to share his reign with the Good Thief. (Luke 23:39–43)
12. Jesus speaks to Mary and the beloved disciple at the foot of the cross. (John 19:25–27)
13. Jesus dies. (Matthew 27:45–50)
14. Jesus is buried. (Matthew 27:61)
15. Jesus is raised from the dead. (Luke 24:1–3)

THE ANGELUS

V. The angel of the Lord declared unto Mary;
R. And she conceived by the Holy Spirit.

Hail Mary, full of grace,
the Lord is with you.
Blessed are you among women
and blessed is the fruit thy womb, Jesus.

Holy Mary, mother of God,
pray for us sinners now
and at the hour of our death.

V. Behold the handmaid of the Lord.
R. Be it done to me according to your word.

Hail Mary . . .

V. And the word was made flesh
R. And dwelt among us.

Hail Mary...

V. Pray for us, O Holy Mother of God,
R. That we may be made worthy of the promises of Christ.

Fill our hearts with your grace, O God:
Through the message of an angel
you have revealed to us the incarnation of your Son;
may his passion and cross
bring us all to the glory of his resurrection.
We ask this through Christ our Lord.

Amen.

THE MYSTERIES OF THE ROSARY

THE JOYFUL MYSTERIES
1. The Annunciation
2. The Visitation
3. The Nativity
4. The Presentation of Jesus at the Temple
5. The Finding of the Child Jesus in the Temple

THE LUMINOUS MYSTERIES
1. The Baptism of the Lord
2. The Wedding at Cana
3. Jesus' Proclamation of the Kingdom of God
4. The Transfiguration
5. The Institution of the Eucharist

THE SORROWFUL MYSTERIES
1. The Agony in the Garden
2. The Scourging at the Pillar
3. The Crowning with Thorns
4. The Carrying of the Cross
5. The Crucifixion

THE GLORIOUS MYSTERIES
1. The Resurrection
2. The Ascension
3. The Descent of the Holy Spirit
4. The Assumption of Mary
5. The Coronation of the Blessed Virgin Mary

THE DIVINE PRAISES

Blessed be God.
Blessed by his holy name.
Blessed be Jesus Christ, true God and true man.
Blessed be the name of Jesus.
Blessed be his most Sacred Heart.
Blessed be his most Precious Blood.
Blessed be Jesus in the most holy sacrament of the altar.
Blessed be the Holy Spirit, the Paraclete.
Blessed be the great Mother of God, Mary most holy.
Blessed be her holy and immaculate conception.
Blessed be her glorious assumption.
Blessed be the name of Mary, virgin and mother.
Blessed be St. Joseph, her most chaste spouse.
Blessed be God in his angels and in his saints.

PRAYERS FOR THE LITURGICAL SEASONS

ADVENT

THE FIRST WEEK OF ADVENT
God,
you are the one who guides, shepherds,
and keeps our lives intact.
Come now,
wake and rouse us
to experience your power and presence.
Take the gifts you have instilled in us
so that we can speak of the hope
that comes from the promise of your Word.

Help us to stay awake and be on the watch for you;
open our eyes to recognize the many signs
of your coming to be with us.
Fill us with kindness to be people of justice,
and help us to pray on behalf of those in need
and those who ache for your loving presence.

Amen.

— *DH*

THE SECOND WEEK OF ADVENT
God,
you alone hold the comfort and tenderness
that we need;
from you we find and know your mercy,
justice, and peace.
Once again,
you call us to be like John the Baptist,
to be your messengers,
to make clear the way for you
and to share the goodness that will be with us.

We have seen the great things that you have done
and continue to do for your people;
when we have drowned in our tears,
you have always taken us by the hand to dry land,
always rejoicing that you are with us,
always, by our side.
We know and believe that our hope
comes from your unending promise.
Help us to keep that hope alive.

Amen.

—DH

IMMACULATE CONCEPTION
God,
you have showered upon all of us
your continual blessings from heaven,
and you have chosen each and every one of us
to be holy.

You have known and loved us
long before we were born,
and we know that you have a plan for us.

Like Mary,
may we always be open to this path
that you have for us.
Help us to respond,
not in fear,
but with faith.

We are your servants.
Let it be done to us as you say.

Amen.

—DH

THE THIRD WEEK OF ADVENT
God,
you are always so faithful to us,
so fair and just,
and always with us.

How can we keep from being happy
and praising you?
We are filled to the brim
with your love and compassion,
and you honor each and every one of us
by your promise to come and dwell with us.

May the lowly ones always sing of your goodness;
may the brokenhearted know your healing;
may those who are imprisoned find new freedom;
and may the task that you have entrusted to each of us
be like your justice,
which always rains down on the meadow,
like the showers that water the earth.

May we rest in you always,
and may we always feel your peace.

Amen.

—DH

THE FOURTH WEEK OF ADVENT
God,
you are the one and only author of our lives,
and we welcome you into our hearts.

How can we possibly approach you
and climb the mountain of your wonder?
How can we possibly stand in your holy place?
As your messengers,
help our hands reach out to those in need,

and free our voices to speak out in blessing.
Seek us out,
so we may seek you,
and may the prayers we speak today
help to fill the longing of our hearts.

Maranatha! Come, Lord Jesus!

Amen.
— DH

CHRISTMAS SEASON

CHRISTMAS
God,
you are the light of the world;
it is so amazing
that you have chosen to become like us,
walk with us,
take on our form,
and be the hope that is beyond
anything we could dream of.

You are with us here!

How can we possibly thank you for such a gift?
How can we sing enough carols,
offer enough praise,
celebrate well and beautifully enough
to match your love for us?

All we can do
is continually to seek you with all our heart,
with everything we have,
with everything we are
and rely on you and open ourselves to your love,
which melts away the chill,
the bitterness,
and the cold
that can still find a home in us.

Come and be born again in our lives;
fire within us "love's pure light."
May this Christmas be the best one yet,
not filled with "presents,"
but rather,
with your "presence."

Amen.

—DH

NEW YEAR'S DAY / MARY, MOTHER OF GOD
God,
as we begin this new year,
we thank you and we praise you.

This new year brings us a new possibility,
another chance,
another opportunity to find a way
to bear you and your mission to the world.

Mary bore your presence,
and she said "yes" to you without hesitation.

We need your help, God,
to begin this year by making her response—
our response:
to live with strength and obedience
and to share humbly
the joy that we feel in our hearts with your people—
who we know are the joy of your heart.

Amen.

—DH

EPIPHANY
God,
as we continue to journey through this season of Christmas,
we want to take the time to celebrate the many ways
you are made known to us.

Please, come
and continue to be our guiding star,
the star of "wonder"
that will lead us to be your people of faith.

May all of us be people of welcome and warmth;
May all of us be people who are your gift to others;
May all of us find the gold, frankincense, and myrrh
that you lay at our feet
and lavish others with its true treasure:
your unconditional love.

Help us to be the people you have called
to be the glory of your light,
your everlasting and piercing star
that lights up the sky of your creation.

Amen.

— DH

LENT

ASH WEDNESDAY
God,
once again you plead for us
to return to you,
for now,
now is the acceptable time.

Come and help us make good use of this time.
Give us the strength to accept
all that is in harmony with following you;
and give us the courage to walk away
from all that keeps us far away from you.
Help us truly to discern the difference.

May we begin this day,
marked with your cross, to become living and breathing signs
of your mercy and reconciliation.

Amen.

— DH

THE FIRST WEEK OF LENT
God,
you are our beginning and our end,
and you bless us here
in giving us this time to reflect on our lives,
not a time to revel in shame, guilt, and pain,
but rather
a time to celebrate fulfillment and growth.

Keep our thoughts on your compassion.
Keep our focus on the message of your Word.
Keep our eyes on what it means
to take up our cross and follow you to all that it means:
suffering—yes;
but also the promise of a new life
that we could never imagine.

Amen.

—DH

THE SECOND WEEK OF LENT
God,
you constantly show and reveal to us
glimpses and previews of your glory and wonder.
And at the same time,
you remind us that we have to keep
living our everyday lives,
lives that more often than not
lead to broken promises.

Help us to hang on to the wonderful "moments"
that you send our way,
always remembering that in each of them
there lies a hope that miracles always lie ahead.

Help us to keep believing that all of these blessings
are signs of what ultimately awaits us.
That being the case,
it really is good to be here with you.

Amen.

—DH

THE THIRD WEEK OF LENT
God,
there is absolutely nothing
that can be kept from you,
for you know us so well,
well beyond how we know ourselves.

May all that happens to us this week
be a source of living water for ourselves
and for each other.
May all the challenges that come our way
lead us to claim you as our God,
our Messiah.
And may every word we speak
and every action we make
proclaim that you are truly
the Savior of the world.

Amen.

—DH

THE FOURTH WEEK OF LENT
God,
we are on an important spiritual journey toward you.
We have no choice on this journey
other than to move forward,
slowly but deliberately toward your light.

May we never forget
that you are sight for all who long to see.
Help us to see better than we do
and to always keep you and your will in our focus.
May everything we say and do
be a partner in showering your compassion,
sinking deep into the hearts of your people.

Amen.

—DH

THE FIFTH WEEK OF LENT
God,
you are so incredible!
You love us so much
that you do not even think twice
about entering into the ugly
and stench-filled tombs of our lives.
You approach our guilt and shame
and help us to discover
a new sense of freedom and peace.

You come toward us, you seek us out,
and you even weep for us when we fail.
You are totally unwilling
to let us stay there;
you pull us out, coming to the rescue,
and liberate everything
that keeps us paralyzed and dead.

Help us to be a similar source of freedom
for all who feel trapped.
May we always be your servants,
leading each other to resurrection.

Amen.

— *DH*

HOLY WEEK

God,
this week we are confronted
with everything that is thrown our way.
It is difficult to understand what it means
to follow the path of Jesus,
especially during this week.

This is the mystery of death and life.
This week we wash each other's feet;
we walk the journey of the passion,
and we ache for the waters of new life.

Keep us attentive this week;
keep us centered on the many mysteries,
the paradoxes,
and the challenges that discipleship brings.

Help us to walk faithfully with Jesus.
Help us to accept and embrace
the journey that has been placed before us.

Amen.

— *DH*

EASTER SEASON

EASTER
God,
this is the day, and this is the time!
You have turned death to life,
sorrow to joy,
darkness to light,
sadness to rejoicing!

You have raised us up from our fears.
You have opened up the graves of despair.
You have freed all of us who feel imprisoned.
You have instilled in the doubting, fresh hope.
You have held the weeping and dried their tears.
You have embraced the shamed and given them healing.
You have taken all our lies and dashed them away.
You have brought all of us to life,
again and again!

We rejoice in you!
Alleluia!

Amen.

— *DH*

PENTECOST
God,
we thank you for the gift
of the Holy Spirit.
We thank you
for the wonderful breath of life
that is the source of passion,
light, and life.

Send down your Spirit upon us,
and break open
the source of your mighty wind
that is the source of all mercy,
kindness, gentleness, and truth.

Come now;
heal our wounds,
and melt away any wall
that may keep us from being peaceful.
Guide our steps; keep us faithful.

May your most Holy Spirit
break open again and again
in our minds and in our hearts.

Amen.

— DH

PRAYERS, MEDITATIONS, AND TOUCHSTONES FROM SCRIPTURE

WHEN I CALL, ANSWER ME

When I call, answer me, O God of justice;
from anguish you released me, have mercy and hear me!

— *Psalm 4:1–2*

DIVINE GLORY AND HUMAN DIGNITY

How great is your name, O Lord our God, through all the earth!

When I see the heavens, the work of your hands,
the moon and the stars that you arranged,
what are we that you should keep us in mind,
mere mortals, that you care for us?

Yet you have made us little less than gods
and crowned us with glory and honor;
you gave us power over the work of your hands,
put all things under our feet.

— *adapted from Psalm 8:2, 4–7*

A PRAYER OF ONE IN ANXIETY

How long, O Lord, will you forget me?
How long will you hide your face?
How long must I bear grief in my soul,
this sorrow in my heart day and night?
How long shall my enemy prevail?

Look at me, answer me, Lord my God!
Give light to my eyes lest I fall asleep in death,
lest my enemy say: "I have prevailed";
lest my foes rejoice to see my fall.

As for me, I trust in your merciful love.
Let my heart rejoice in your saving help.
Let me sing to you Lord for your goodness to me,
sing psalms to your name, O Lord, Most High.

—*Psalm 13*

TRUE HAPPINESS

O Lord, it is you who are my portion and cup,
it is you yourself who are my prize.

I keep you, Lord, ever in my sight;
since you are at my right hand, I shall stand firm.

And so my heart rejoices, my soul is glad;
even my body shall rest in safety.
For you will not leave my soul among the dead,
nor let your beloved know decay.

You will show me the path of life,
the fullness of joy in your presence,
at your right hand happiness forever.

—*Psalm 16:5, 8–11*

YOU ARE MY SHEPHERD

Lord, you are my shepherd;
there is nothing I shall want.
Fresh and green are the pastures
where you give me repose.
Near restful waters you lead me,
to revive my drooping spirit.

You guide me along the right path;
You are true to your name.
If I should walk in the valley of darkness
no evil would I fear.

You are there with your crook and your staff;
with these you give me comfort.

You have prepared a banquet for me
in the sight of my foes.
My head you have anointed with oil;
my cup is overflowing.

Surely goodness and kindness shall follow me
all the days of my life.
In the Lord's own house shall I dwell
forever and ever.

— *Psalm 23*

A PRAYER FOR GUIDANCE AND PROTECTION

To you, O Lord, I lift up my soul.

Lord, make me know your ways,
Lord, teach me your paths.
Make me walk in your truth, and teach me,
for you are God my savior.

The Lord is good and upright,
showing the path to those who stray,
guiding the humble in the right path,
and teaching the way to the poor.

— *Psalm 25:1, 4–5, 8–9*

TRUST IN A TIME OF AFFLICTION

The Lord is my light and my help;
whom shall I fear?
The Lord is the stronghold of my life;
before whom shall I shrink?

There is one thing I ask of the Lord,
for this I long,
to live in the house of the Lord,
all the days of my life,
to savor the sweetness of the Lord,
to behold his temple.

I am sure I shall see the Lord's goodness
in the land of the living.
In the Lord, hold firm and take heart.
Hope in the Lord!

— *Psalm 27:1, 4, 13–14*

MY SOUL IS THIRSTING FOR GOD

Like the deer that yearns
for running streams,
so my soul is yearning
for you, my God.

My soul is thirsting for God,
the God of my life;
when can I enter and see
the face of God?

— *Psalm 42:2–3*

A PURE HEART

A pure heart create for me, O God,
put a steadfast spirit within me.
Do not cast me away from your presence,
nor deprive me of your holy spirit.
Give me again the joy of your help;
with a spirit of fervor sustain me.

— *Psalm 51:12–14*

GOD, THE ROCK OF STRENGTH

In God alone is my soul at rest;
from God comes my help.
God alone is my rock, my stronghold,
my fortress; I stand firm.

— *Psalm 62:2–3*

YOU WILL NOT FEAR

You will not fear the terror of the night
nor the arrow that flies by day.

A thousand may fall at your side,
ten thousand fall at your right,
you, it will never approach;
God's faithfulness is buckler and shield.

Upon you no evil shall fall,
no plague approach where you dwell.
For you God has commanded the angels,
to keep you in all your ways.

— *Psalm 91:5–7, 10–11*

BLESS THE LORD

Bless the Lord, my soul!
All that is within me and around me,
bless the holy name of God!

Do not forget God's blessings,
who forgives our shortcomings,
who heals us from our disease,
who redeems us from the pit,
who crowns us with unending love and mercy,
who satisfies us with good as long as we live,
so that we may always have
the youth and energy of an eagle!

The Lord is mercy and graciousness,
slow to anger,
abounding always in love.
God will not accuse
or keep anger forever.
The Lord will not deal with us
according to our sins,
for God does not haunt us
with our sins.
As high as the heavens are above the earth,
this is the grandness of the Lord's love for us.
As far as the east is from the west,

this is the vastness of the Lord's mercy for us
when we fall.
As a father and mother have compassion
for their children,
in the same way the Lord
has compassion for us who show honor.

Bless the Lord, my soul!

— *adapted from Psalm 103:1–5, 8–13*

THE NAME OF GOD

How can I make a return
for the goodness of God?
This saving cup I will bless and sing,
and call the name of God!

The dying of those who keep faith
is precious to our God.
I am your servant, called from your hands,
you have set me free!

To you I will offer my thanks
and call upon your name.
You are my promise for all to see:
I love your name, O God!

— *adapted from Psalm 116:12–18*

THE LORD, OUR PROTECTOR

I lift up my eyes to the mountains;
from where shall come my help?
My help shall come from the Lord
who made heaven and earth.

The Lord is your guard and your shade;
and stands at your right.
By day the sun shall not smite you
nor the moon in the night.

The Lord will guard you from evil,
and will guard your soul.
The Lord will guard your going and coming
both now and forever.

— *Psalm 121:1–2, 5–8*

LIKE A LITTLE CHILD

Like a little child in its mother's arms,
my soul will rest in you.

— *adapted from Psalm 131:2b*

BEFORE I WAS BORN

You made me, you formed me,
you kept me alive long before I was born.

You have sought me out and found me;
you know where I sit or stand.
You know the depths of my heart,
whenever I move or rest,
you find me wherever I am.

Before the word comes from my mouth,
you know what I want to stay.
You come close to me,
you lay your hand upon me.
All of this is too much for me.

How can I ever hide from you?
Where can I run from you?
Above and below—you are there.
To the dawn or to the sea—you are there.
Your hand will guide my way.

You have created every inch of me,
you have knit me to my mother's womb.
You have record of all my days,
long before they ever began.
How amazing your thoughts, O God.

— *adapted from Psalm 139:1–10, 13, 16b–17*

THE TRUE SECURITY

My child,
do not let these escape from your sight:
keep sound wisdom and prudence,
and they will be life for your soul
and adornment for your neck.
Then you will walk on your way securely
and your foot will not stumble.
If you sit down, you will not be afraid;
when you lie down, your sleep will be sweet.
Do not be afraid of sudden panic,
or of the storm that strikes the wicked;
for the Lord will be your confidence
and will keep your foot from being caught.

Do not withhold good from those
to whom it is due,
when it is your power to do it.

Do not plan harm against your neighbor
who lives trustingly beside you.
Do not quarrel with anyone without cause,
when no harm has been done to you.
Do not envy the violent
and do not choose any of their ways.

— *Proverbs 3:21–27, 29–31*

EVERYTHING HAS ITS TIME

For everything there is a season,
and a time for every matter under heaven:
a time to be born, and a time to die;
a time to plant, and a time to pluck up what is planted;
a time to kill, and a time to heal;
a time to break down, and a time to build up;
a time to weep, and a time to laugh;
a time to mourn, and a time to dance;
a time to throw away stones, and a time to gather stones together;
a time to embrace, and a time to refrain from embracing;
a time to seek, and a time to lose;
a time to keep, and a time to throw away;
a time to tear, and a time to sew;

a time to keep silence, and a time to speak;
a time to love, and a time to hate;
a time for war, and a time for peace.

— *Ecclesiastes 3:1–8*

A FUTURE WITH HOPE

For surely I know the plans I have for you,
says the Lord,
plans for your welfare and not for harm,
to give you a future with hope.

— *adapted from Jeremiah 29:11*

I WILL BE YOUR GOD

You shall be my people,
and I will be your God.

— *Jeremiah 30:22*

I WILL POUR OUT MY SPIRIT

I will pour out my spirit on everyone;
your sons and daughters will prophesy,
the old ones will dream dreams,
and the young shall see visions.

— *adapted from Joel 2:28*

IF GOD IS FOR US

If God is for us, who is against us?

— *Romans 8:31b*

NOTHING CAN SEPARATE US

For I am convinced that neither death,
nor life,
nor angels, nor rulers,
nor things present,
nor things to come,
nor powers,
nor height, nor depth,
nor anything else in all creation,
will be able to separate us from the love of God
through Christ Jesus our Lord.

— *Romans 8:38–39*

GOD'S LOVE

Hope does not disappoint us,
because God's love has been poured into our hearts
through the Holy Spirit that has been given to us.

— *Romans 5:5*

MANY GIFTS

There are a varieties of gifts, but the same Spirit;
and there are varieties of services, but the same Lord;
and there are varieties of activities,
but it is the same God who activates all of them in everyone.
To each is given the manifestation of the Spirit
for the common good.

— *1 Corinthians 12:3–7*

LOVE

Love is patient; love is kind;
love is not envious or boastful or arrogant or rude.
It does not insist on its own way;
It is not irritable or resentful;
It does not rejoice in wrongdoing,
but rejoices in the truth.
It bears all things, believes all things,

hopes all things, endures all things.
Love never ends.

— *1 Corinthians 13:4–8a*

YOU ARE OUR LETTER

You are our letter,
written on our hearts to be known and read by all,
written not with ink, but with the Spirit of the living God,
not on tablets of stone
but on tablets of human hearts.

— *adapted from 2 Corinthians 3:2–3*

NO LONGER STRANGERS

So then you are no longer strangers or aliens,
but you are citizens with the saints
and also members of the household of God.

— *Ephesians 2:19*

LET YOUR GENTLENESSSS BE KNOWN

Let your gentleness be known,
so all may know the Lord is near.
Do not worry; reach out to God in prayer.
Stay with all that you have learned
and all that you have heard and seen,
and the peace of God will be with you.

— *adapted from Philippians 4:4–9*

DEVOTE YOURSELVES TO PRAYER

Devote yourselves to prayer,
keeping alert in it with thanksgiving.

— *Colossians 4:2*

WHOEVER SPEAKS

Whoever speaks must do so
as one speaking the very words of God;
whoever serves must do so
with the strength that God supplies,
so that God may be glorified in all things
through Jesus Christ.

— 1 Peter 4:11

PRAYERS, MEDITATIONS, AND CHALLENGES FROM THE WISDOM COMMUNITY

BEHOLD GOD

Behold God,
consider God.
contemplate God,
and desire to imitate God.

— *DH (inspired from a prayer of Saint Clare)*

NADA DE TURBE

Let nothing come now and frighten you.
All things must pass—God never changes.
When you have God,
nothing more is needed;
for God alone is enough.

— *DH (adapted from a prayer of Saint Therese of Avila)*

PRAYER OF SAINT PATRICK

Christ be with me,
Christ before me,
Christ behind me,
Christ on my right,
Christ on my left,
Christ where I lie,
Christ where I sit,
Christ where I arise.

Christ in the heart of everyone who thinks of me,
Christ in the mouth of everyone who speaks of me,
Christ in every eye that sees me,
Christ in every ear that hears me.

— *Saint Patrick*

GOD'S CAUSE

God's cause
is the only concern of our hearts.

— *Theresa Gerhardinger*

PRAYER FOR GENEROSITY

Lord,
teach me to be generous.
Teach me to serve you as you deserve,
to give and not to count the cost,
to fight and not to heed the wounds,
to toil and not to seek for rest,
to labor and not to ask for reward,
save that of knowing that I do your will.

— *Saint Ignatius of Loyola*

THE ONLY NECESSARY THING

Prayer is the center of the Christian life.
It is the only necessary thing.
It is living with God here and now.

— *Henri J. M. Nouwen in* The Only Necessary Thing: Living a Prayerful Life

THE LIGHT WITHIN YOU

The more light you allow within you,
the brighter the world you live in will be.

— *Shakti Gawain*

OUTSIDE YOUR COMFORT ZONE

If your prayer is not enticing you outside your comfort zones,
if your Christ is not an occasional "threat,"
you probably need to do some growing up and learning to love.

— *Richard Rohr in* Everything Belongs: The Gift of Contemplative Prayer

LOVE EACH OTHER

Love each other as God loves each one of you,
with an intense and particular love.
Be kind to each other:
It is better to commit faults with gentleness
than to work miracles with unkindness.

— *Mother Teresa of Calcutta*

FRIENDSHIP

Friendship is the source of the greatest pleasures,
and without friends even the most agreeable pursuits
    become tedious.

—*Saint Thomas Aquinas*

DO NOT LOOK TO TOMORROW

Do not look forward to what may happen tomorrow.
The same Everlasting Father,
who takes care of you today,
will take care of you tomorrow
and every day.

— *Saint Francis de Sales*

THE PURPOSE OF PRAYER

The purpose of the exploration of prayer
is not to get anywhere . . .
We cannot attain the presence of God
because we're already totally in the presence of God.
What's absent is awareness.

— *Richard Rohr in* Everything Belongs: The Gift of Contemplative Prayer

PRAYERS AND LOVE

Prayers and love are learned in the hour
when prayer has become impossible
and your heart has turned to stone.

— *Thomas Merton*

ABIDE, O SPIRIT OF LIFE

May peace fill our hearts,
may love fill our minds;
make us loving disciples of Christ.
So may we be one,
so may we be yours:
abide, O Spirit of Life!

— *Bill Huebsch (adapted from a prayer by Pope John XXIII)*

TO BE REALLY HAPPY

I don't know what your destiny will be,
but one thing I know:
the only ones among you who will be really happy
are those who have sought and found how to serve.

— *Albert Schweitzer*

WHAT DOES GOD REQUIRE?

God does not require the martyrdom of the body;
he requires only the martyrdom of the heart and the will.

— *Saint John Vianney*

PERFECT CHARITY

Most high, glorious God,
enlighten the darkness of my heart;
give me right faith,
sure hope,
and perfect charity.
Fill me with understanding
and knowledge,
that I may fulfill your command.

— *DH (adapted from the "Prayer Before the Cross" by Saint Francis of Assisi)*

OUR DESIRE FOR GOD

Our desire for God is the desire
that should guide all other desires.

— *Henri J. M. Nouwen in* The Only Necessary Thing: Living a Prayerful Life

JESUS NEEDS US

The Risen Christ is with us today,
and he continues to need each one of you.
Jesus needs your eyes to continue to see.
He needs your strength to continue to work.
He needs your voice to continue to teach.
He needs your hands to continue to bless.
He needs your heart to continue to love.
And Jesus needs your whole being
to continue to build his body, the Church.
As we believe, so let us live!

— *Joseph Bernardin in* The Gift of Peace: Personal Reflections

THE GREAT AND MERCIFUL SURPRISE

The great and merciful surprise
is that we come to God not by doing it right
but by doing it wrong.

— *Richard Rohr in* Everything Belongs: The Gift of Contemplative Prayer

EVERYTHING IS A MIRACLE

There are two ways to live your life.
One is as though nothing is a miracle.
The other is as though everything is a miracle.

— *Albert Einstein*

TAKE CHRIST

If, then, you are looking for the way by which you should go, take Christ, because he himself is the way.

— *Saint Thomas Aquinas*

TOLERANCE

O Lord, help me not to despise or oppose
what I do not understand.

— *William Penn*

THE CHRISTIAN MUST REMEMBER

The Christian must remember
that he is likely to be
the only copy of the gospels
that the non-Christian will ever see.

— *Philip Scharper*

TO HEAL

Whatever house I enter,
I shall come to heal.

— *adapted from the Hippocratic Oath*

I HAVE FOUND MYSELF

I thank God for my handicaps, for through them
I have found myself, my work, and my God.

— *Helen Keller*

THE SERENITY PRAYER

God,
grant me the serenity
to accept the things I cannot change,
courage to change the things I can,
and wisdom to know the difference.

Living one day at a time;
enjoying one moment at a time;
accepting hardship as a way to peace;
taking, as Jesus did,
this sinful world as it is,
not as I would have it;
trusting that you will make all things right
if I surrender to your will,
so that I may be reasonably happy in this life
and supremely happy with you in the next.

— *Reinhold Niebuhr (adapted)*

THAT I MAY SEE

Lord,
grant that I may see,
that I may see you,
that I may see and experience you present
and animating all things.
Jesus, help me to perfect the perception
and expression of my vision.
Help me to the right action,
the right word;
help me to give the example
that will reveal you the best.

— *Pierre Teilhard de Chardin in* Hymn of the Universe

FORGIVENESS

We need to forgive and be forgiven every day,
every hour—unceasingly.

— *Henri J. M. Nouwen in* The Only Necessary Thing: Living a Prayerful Life

SCOOPING UP THE DUST

Love is the person of the resurrection,
scooping up the dust and chanting, "live!"

— *Emily Dickinson*

YOUR FUTURE

Your future depends on many things,
but mostly on you.

— *Frank Tyger*

PRAYER OF SAINT IGNATIUS

Take, O Lord,
and receive all my liberty,
my memory,
my understanding,
and all my will,
all that I have and possess.
You have given all of these to me;
to you I restore them.
All are yours,
dispose of them all according to your will.
Give me only your love and your grace;
having these I will be rich enough
and will ask for nothing more.

— *Saint Ignatius of Loyola*

TO BECOME WHAT HE IS

Christ became what we are
in order that we might become what he is.

— *Saint Athanasius*

TAKE ME FROM MYSELF

Lord, take me from myself
and give me to yourself.

— *Saint Catherine of Siena*

HOLY SPIRIT PRAYER

Breathe in me, O Holy Spirit,
that my thoughts may all be holy;
act in me, O Holy Spirit,
that my work, too, may be holy;
draw my heart, O Holy Spirit,
that I love only what is holy.
Strengthen me, O Holy Spirit,
to defend all that is holy;
guard me, then, O Holy Spirit,
that I always may be holy.

— *Saint Augustine*

DOING HIS JOURNEY

It seems that we Christians
have been worshiping Jesus' journey
instead of doing his journey.

— *Richard Rohr in* Everything Belongs: The Gift of Contemplative Prayer

GRATITUDE

If the only prayer we ever prayed
was "thank you," that would be enough.

— *Meister Eckhart*

THE LIGHT OF CHRIST

The light of Christ surrounds us,
the love of Christ enfold us.
The power of Christ protects us,
the presence of Christ watches over us.

— *adapted from a prayer by James Dillet Freeman*

A LOVE LETTER

I am a little pencil
in the hands of a writing God
who is sending a love letter to the world.

— *Mother Teresa of Calcutta*

GOD'S INITIATIVE

I am deeply convinced that the necessity to pray,
and to pray unceasingly,
is not so much based on our desire for God
as on God's desire for us.
It is God's passionate pursuit of us
that calls us to prayer.
Prayer comes from God's initiative, not ours.
It might sound shocking,
but it is biblical to say:
God wants us more than we want God!

— *Henri J. M. Nouwen in* The Only Necessary Thing: Living a Prayerful Life

THE LONG LONELINESS

We cannot love God unless we love each other,
and to love we must know each other.
We know him in the breaking of the bread,
and we know each other in the breaking of the bread,

and we are not alone anymore.
Heaven is a banquet, and life is a banquet too,
even with a crust, where there is companionship.

We have all known the long loneliness,
and we have learned that the only solution is love
and that love comes from community.

— *Dorothy Day in* The Long Loneliness: The Autobiography of Dorothy Day

CREATE JOY

Life will bring you pain all by itself.
Your responsibility is to create joy.

— *Milton Erickson*

TRUE PRAYER

True prayer . . . nips the lie in the bud.
It is usually experienced as tears,
surrender, or forgiveness.

— *Richard Rohr in* Everything Belongs: The Gift of Contemplative Prayer

I HAVE ONLY TODAY

My life is an instant, an hour which passes by;
my life is a moment which I have no power to stay.
You know, O my God,
that to love you here on earth—
I have only today.

— *Saint Thérèse of Lisieux*

VOICE IN MY SILENCE

I believe that God is in me
as the sun is in the color and fragrance
of a flower—
the Light in my darkness,
the Voice in my silence.

— *Helen Keller*

LET IT SPRING FROM LOVE

The thought manifests itself as the word;
the word manifests itself as the deed;
the deed develops into habit;
and habit hardens into character.
So watch the thought and its ways with care,
and let it spring from love
born out of concern for all beings.

— *The Buddha*

SOMEBODY HELPED YOU

No matter what accomplishments you achieve,
somebody helped you.

— *Althea Gibson*

WORK AND PRAY

Work as if everything depends on you.
Pray as if everything depends on God.

— *Saint Ignatius of Loyola*

MY OWN HEART

The things that hurt me the most
are found in my own thoughts,
my own mind,
my own heart.

— *DH*

DARE TO LOVE

Dare to love and to be a real friend.
The love you give and receive
is a reality that will lead you closer and closer to God
as well as to those whom God
has given you to love.

— *Henri J. M. Nouwen in* The Inner Voice of Love

MORE THAN EVER

More than ever I find myself in the hands of God.
This is what I have wanted all my life from my youth.

But now there is a difference;
the initiative is entirely with God.

It is indeed a profound spiritual experience
to know and feel myself so totally in God's hands.

— *Pedro Arrupe (written after he suffered a stroke) in* One Jesuit's Spiritual Journey: Autobiographical Conversations with Jean-Claude Dietsch

OUR OWN CENTER

We do not find our own center; it finds us.
Our own mind will not be able to figure it out.

— *Richard Rohr in* Everything Belongs: The Gift of Contemplative Prayer

JUST TO BE, JUST TO LIVE

Just to be is a blessing.
Just to live is holy

— *Rabbi Abraham Herschel*

WITHOUT PRAYER

A spiritual life without prayer
is like the Gospel without Christ.

— *Henri J. M. Nouwen in* The Only Necessary Thing: Living a Prayerful Life

PRAYERS FOR VARIOUS OCCASIONS AND CIRCUMSTANCES

BEGINNING OF THE YEAR FOR TEACHERS AND CATECHISTS

God,
we greet you
and welcome this time of beginnings
with hope and gratitude.
We thank you for the call and gift
to teach and lead;
we thank you for the honor
to share our knowledge and skill;
we thank you for the precious opportunity
that lies before us this year.

Come and bless us;
help us to rejoice in the students
whom you have entrusted to our care.
Help us to do more than teach;
help us to guide and mentor
these wonderful works of art,
to learn, to discover, to imagine,
and to dream.

May we be messengers
of knowledge, learning, possibilities, and wonder—
all in the spirit of your marvelous love and mercy.

Bless us, and give us the energy,
courage, and insight that we need.

Amen.

—*DH*

A PRAYER FOR TEACHERS AND CATECHISTS

O Lord Jesus Christ,
you have laid your hands on us,
you have called us by name,
you have commanded us:
"Go, teach all nations."
We ask you: put your love into our hearts.
Put your understanding into our minds;
put your words into our mouths.
May we always raise and serve you,
who live and reign with the Father and the Holy Spirit,
one God forever and ever.

Amen.

— *Nigerian Catechists' Prayer*

BEGINNING OF THE YEAR FOR YOUTH

God,
we greet you and welcome this time of beginnings
with joy, excitement, anxiety, worry,
and a bit of hesitation.
We thank you for the blessings of summer fun and rest;
we thank you for bringing us together again with our friends;
and we thank you for the many things,
known and unknown,
that await us this year.
We also come a bit nervous,
concerned about the challenges that lie ahead,
the potential stress and unknown mountains
that we may be asked to climb.

Regardless of what we are feeling—
we surrender all our concerns to your care and attention.

Be with us this year.
Walk with us into the known and unknown,
and give us the courage we need to tackle
whatever comes our way;
and bring us the joy to celebrate
the wonders and opportunities that are in store for us.

Bless our minds, our thoughts,
our critical thinking, and the growth that is given to us—
if we are willing to accept and say "yes."

Bless us, God, and be with us.

Amen.

— *DH*

TO BEGIN A CLASS OR MEETING

O Spirit of God,
we ask you to help orient all our actions
by your inspirations.
Carry them on by your gracious assistance,
that every prayer and work of ours
may always begin from you
and through you be happily ended.

— *Anonymous*

WHEN I AM ANXIOUS OR STRESSED

God,
help me to slow down,
to breathe deeply,
to think simply,
to pray softly and gently.

Stop the rush of fear,
and replenish it with your peace.

Then my heart can create anew.

— *DH*

WHEN THERE IS CONFLICT

God,
things are not good right now.

My friend and I are not talking to one another,
and the lines are being drawn.

We need some healing.

Please come
and help us to soften the hardness
that we are holding deep inside
and toward each other.

Help us to hear each other.
Help us to listen to each other.
Help us both not to be about
"winning or losing,"
but rather
to reach out to one another with care,
love, and respect.

Help us to nurture and lift each other up
and not to destroy each other.

Amen.

—DH

WHEN THERE ARE DISTRACTIONS

God,
I cannot seem to clear my head,
for there are distractions everywhere.
There are noises around,
and I feel preoccupied with things
beyond myself.
I have so many worries;
there is stress at home,
at school, in my work,
and there is just too much to do.

Help me to accept and tolerate
these distractions
and to remember that I am human.

Help me to be gentle with myself
and let the distractions fall away,
and then, hopefully,
I will see only you.

Then my path will be clearer
and my attitude more peaceful.

—DH

BEFORE A TEST

God,
here I am,
prepared or not well prepared.
Either way,
I need your presence with me
to be focused, to be calm,
and to have a mind clear of distractions.

If I am anxious—
help me to stop and breathe deeply.
If I am overconfident—
help me not to take anything for granted.

Just be with me,
and guide my thinking
as I determine answers and choices.
Help me remember what I have learned
not just to do well on the test
but to really let it sink in
and help inform all that I am.

I thank you for being here with me
right here, right now,
regardless of the outcome.

Amen.

—DH

AFTER A TEST

God,
well, it is over.
Maybe I did well, or maybe I did not.
Regardless, it is over now,
and I need to move on.
Help me not to become too preoccupied
or let what just happened
completely drown out everything else
that lies before me today.
It is over;
hopefully I did my best,
and no matter how it all turns out,
it will not be the last word of what I know,
or who I am.

Help me to remember that.

Amen.

—*DH*

THANK YOU FOR MY FRIENDS

God,
I am so thankful to you
that you have blest me with such good friends.

It easy to take them for granted,
and not always to treasure them,
affirm them,
or say "thank you" to them
when they are there for me,
when they show their friendship.

Help me to remember
to hold each of them as precious,
and also to remember
that, like me,
they are not perfect.
Sometimes they will not always live up
to my expectations;
sometimes they will make choices

that I do not understand
or approve of.
But, nonetheless, they are my friends,
and I want to be faithful and forgiving of them,
as you, God,
always are for me.

Thanks again for these wonderful friends:
human, wonderful, imperfect, generous,
faithful, fragile, and utterly fantastic—
because they are just like me;
they are created from your hands.

Amen.

—DH

WHEN A RELATIONSHIP BREAKS UP

God,
this is so painful.
I am not sure how I feel right now—
I feel disoriented, angry, hurt,
sad, or maybe even relieved;
I don't know.

While I may think I know the reasons
why this happened, it is still hard.
While it may be the best thing for the two of us,
it is still hard.
While it might not have been the healthiest relationship
it is still hard.
It may have been a wonderful relationship,
and one that I do not want to lose right now.

Regardless of the circumstances,
I need you, God, to help me make sense of it all
and to find the footing to keep moving.
I have to remember that it may take some time
to get over this,
and it will probably be the same for the other person.

I pray for both of us, God,
even if the other person really hurt me.
I know that both of us need your help
and guidance during this time,
which still feels raw and painful.

Be with us—that is the most important thing
that we need right now:
your presence, your acceptance,
and your love.

Amen.

—*DH*

WHEN IT IS HARD TO FORGIVE

God,
right now at this moment,
the last thing I want to do is forgive.

I am mad, I am angry,
I feel betrayed, hurt,
and I feel I was treated badly.

I do not want other people—or even you—
to tell me that I need to let go, forgive,
or not to hang on to my hurt.
Right now,
I really want to hang on to it—

I feel justified,
and I want the other person
to feel what I am feeling,
I want to hurt them back;
I want revenge.
I do not like having these feelings,
but they are real for me right now.

It is hard to do so,
but God,
I want to lay these feelings before you.
Even though I am angry,
I know I need at some point

not to let this consume me,
and to find a way to forgive.

Help me, God.
Help me to work through
all that I am feeling,
knowing that someday,
after a time,
you will heal the wounds,
and then I will be able to finally
reach out and heal the rift
and pain toward the other.

Help me.

Amen.

— *DH*

A BIRTHDAY PRAYER AND BLESSING

God,
we thank you for (name);
for his/her life;
for the journey of years
that have come to this moment.

We thank you for how he/she
has been a part of our lives,
for the good and fun times,
and for how he/she has made our lives better
for being with us.

Be with her/him today
to celebrate well
and to look forward to many,
many birthdays and good times ahead.

Amen.

— *DH*

FOR THE GIFT OF HOSPITALITY AND WELCOME

God,
open the doors wide,
unlock the barriers
of my apathy,
my judgment,
and my fear.

Set me free from my place of comfort
to go out of my way,
to inconvenience myself,
to leave the safety of my own world.

Bless me once again
with the gift you have given me;
outstretch your loving embrace
through my own arms
to welcome those whom you call your children.

Help my eyes be your eyes,
to awaken the weary,
that I may see the wonderful treasure
that they are
and give freely
the gifts that you have given to me.

May I welcome others,
as you have welcomed me
again and again,
as the eternal, impeccable host.

May it never be the case
that there be strangers in this place.

— DH

WHEN A FAMILY MEMBER OR FRIEND DIES

God,
I feel so lost
and so unbelievably angry right now.
I am angry at you.
How could you let this happen?

You,
the one I have been taught to believe
is so loving,
so caring,
so "on my side" in everything that I do—
why can't you fix this?
I am sorry,
but all of the talk of "resurrection,"
"new life," and "eternal life"
does not seem to offer any comfort right now.

Yet,
in the midst of this,
I am still trying to hold on to my faith in you—
just barely,
hanging on by my fingernails,
I am wanting to believe
that somewhere in the midst of all of this,
you have a plan.
Come now,
and help me more than ever
to believe in that plan.
Everything in the Scriptures says
that death will not win out,
that you are about life,
life to the full.
Come now,
and reveal that hope to me,
and strengthen in me the will
to keep moving forward,
to keep believing in you,
to keep attentive to the signs
around me
that proclaim you still exist,
that your love is stronger than death.

Help me to remember
the wonderful things about
this human life
that have blest me so deeply.
Help me to remember
that in the midst of life,
you were there;

and help me also to remember
that you are still with me
even in the midst of this absence.

Stay with me,
and walk with me in the midst
of this awful journey.
Help me get to the other side,
so I can rejoice again
in your promise of life.
Live everlasting.

Amen.

—*DH*

ETERNAL REST

Eternal rest grant to them, O Lord,
and let perpetual light shine upon them.
May they rest in peace.

Amen.

PRAYERS AND MEDITATONS FOR PEACE, COMPASSION, AND JUSTICE

PRAYER FOR PEACE

Peace before us, peace behind us,
peace under our feet.
Peace within us, peace over us,
let all around us be peace.

— *DH (inspired by a Navajo prayer)*

PRAYER OF SAINT FRANCIS

Lord, make me an instrument of your peace;
where there is hatred, let me sow love;
where there is injury, pardon;
where there is doubt, faith;
where there is despair, hope;
where there is darkness, light;
and where there is sadness, joy.

Grant that I may not so much seek
to be consoled as to console;
to be understood, as to understand,
to be loved as to love;
for it is in giving that we receive,
it is in pardoning that we are pardoned,
and it is in dying that we are born into eternal life.

— *attributed to Saint Francis of Assisi*

PEACE

Peace is not the product of terror or fear.
Peace is not the silence of cemeteries.
Peace is not the silent result of violent repression.
Peace is the generous,
tranquil contribution of all to the good of all.
Peace is dynamism. Peace is generosity.
It is right and it is duty.

— *Oscar Romero in* The Violence of Love: The Pastoral Wisdom of Archbishop Oscar Romero

IF YOU WANT PEACE

If you want peace,
work for justice.

— *Pope Paul VI*

WHAT DOES LOVE LOOK LIKE?

What does love look like?
It has feet to go to the needy.
It has eyes to see misery and want.
It has ears to hear the sighs and sorrows of others.

— *Saint Augustine*

SPEAK OUT

Speak out for those who cannot speak,
for the rights of the destitute.
Speak out, judge righteously,
defend the rights of the poor and needy.

— *Proverbs 31:8–9*

A YEAR OF FAVOR

The spirit of the Lord is upon me,
because the Lord has anointed me;
he has sent me to bring good news to the oppressed,
to bind up the brokenhearted,

to proclaim liberty to the captives,
and release to the prisoners;
to proclaim a year of the Lord's favor.

— *Isaiah 61:1–2a*

THE BEATITUDES

"Blessed are the poor in spirit, for theirs is the kingdom
 of heaven.
Blessed are those who mourn, for they will be comforted.
Blessed are the meek, for they will inherit the earth.
Blessed are those who hunger and thirst for righteousness,
 for they will be filled.
Blessed are the merciful, for they will receive mercy.
Blessed are the pure of heart, for they will see God.
Blessed are the peacemakers, for they will be called children
 of God.
Blessed are those who are persecuted for righteousness' sake,
 for theirs is the kingdom of heaven.
Blessed are you when people revile you and persecute you
and utter all kinds of evil against you falsely on my account.
Rejoice and be glad, for your reward is great in heaven."

— *Matthew 5:3–12a*

CALLING GOD

You may call God love,
you may call God goodness.
But the best name for God is compassion.

— *Meister Eckhart*

OUR ONLY HOPE

Our only hope today
lies in our ability to recapture the revolutionary spirit
and go out into a sometimes hostile world
declaring eternal hostility
to poverty, racism, and militarism.

— *Martin Luther King, Jr.*

THE CAPACITY OF CHANGE

Are you willing to believe
that even though they are guilty of a diabolical act,
they still continue to be children of God,
not monsters, not demons,
but those with the capacity to change?

— *Desmond Tutu*

THE TIME HAS COME

The time for healing of the wounds has come.
The time to build is upon us.
We pledge ourselves to liberate all our people
from the continuing bondage of poverty, deprivation,
suffering, gender, and other discrimination.
There is no easy road to freedom.
None of us acting alone can achieve success.
We must, therefore, act together as a united people,
for reconciliation, for nation building,
for the birth of a new world.

— *Nelson Mandela*

IN SPITE OF EVERYTHING

In spite of everything, I still believe
that people are really good at heart.
I simply can't build up my hopes on a foundation
consisting of confusion, misery, and death.
I see the world gradually being turned into a wilderness;
I hear the ever-approaching thunder, which will destroy us too;
I can feel the suffering of millions;
and yet if I look up into the heavens,
I think that it will all come right,
that this cruelty will end,
and that peace and tranquility will return again.
In the meantime, I must uphold my ideals,
for perhaps the time will come
when I shall be able to carry them out.

— *Anne Frank in* The Diary of a Young Girl

SEEK TRUTH

Compelled by the Gospel,
outraged by injustice,
and stirred by the Wisdom of God:

Seek truth, make peace,
reverence life.

— vision statement, the Adrian Dominican Sisters

WHEN AND HOW?

Blessed are those who hunger and thirst after justice,
for they shall be satisfied.
But when, O Lord, and how?

— Edicio de la Torre

MAKE US WORTHY, LORD

Make us worthy, Lord,
to serve others throughout the world
who live and die
in poverty or hunger.
Give them, through our hands,
this day their daily bread,
and by our understanding love,
give peace and joy.

— Mother Teresa of Calcutta

CONTACT WITH THE POOR

We need to accept that one of the spiritual disciplines —
just like reading the Scriptures and praying and liturgy —
is physical contact with the poor.
It is an essential ingredient.
If we are never in their presence,
if we never eat with them,
if we never hear their stories,
if we are always separated from them,
then I think something really vital is missing.

— Sister Helen Prejean, CSJ

SPEAK OUT

Speak out for those who cannot speak,
for the rights of all the destitute.
Speak out, judge righteously,
defend the rights of the poor and needy.

— *Proverbs 31:8–9*

WHAT GOSPEL?

A church that doesn't provoke any crises,
a gospel that doesn't unsettle,
a word of God that doesn't get under anyone's skin,
a word of God that doesn't touch the real sin
of the society in which it is being proclaimed—
what gospel is that?

— *Oscar Romero in* The Violence of Love: The Pastoral Wisdom of Archbishop Oscar Romero

THE PROBLEM

The problem, unstated until now,
is how to live in a damaged world
where pain is meant to be gagged, uncured, ungrieved over.
The problem is to connect, without hysteria,
the pain of anyone's body with the pain of the world's body.

— *Adrienne Rich*

CHRIST HAS NO BODY NOW ON EARTH

Christ has no body now on earth but yours;
yours are the only hands
with which he can do his work,
yours are the only feet
with which he can go about the world,
yours are the only eyes
through which his compassion can shine forth
upon a troubled world.
Christ has no body on earth now but yours.

— *Saint Therese of Avila*

WHERE GOD IS

The guarantee of one's prayer
is not in saying a lot of words.
The guarantee of one's petition is very easy to know:
How do I treat the poor?
Because that is where God is.
The degree in which you approach them,
and the love with which you approach them,
or the scorn with which you approach them—
that is how you approach your God.
What you do to them, you do to God.
The way you look at them is the way you look at God.

— *Oscar Romero in* The Violence of Love: The Pastoral Wisdom of Archbishop Oscar Romero

GOD'S WORK

Those who do not share power
are not about God's work.

— *Megan McKenna*

WORLD PEACE PRAYER

Lead us from death to life,
from falsehood to truth.
Lead us from despair to hope,
from fear to trust.
Let peace fill our hearts,
our world, our universe.
Let us dream together,
pray together,
work together,
to build one world
of peace and justice for all.

— *Anonymous*

MARY, QUEEN OF PEACE

Mary, Queen of Peace,
we entrust our lives to you.
Shelter us from war, hatred, and oppression.
Teach us to live in peace,
to educate ourselves for peace.
Inspire us to act justly,
to revere all that God has made.
Root peace firmly in our hearts
and in our world.

Amen.

— *Pax Christi*

THE NATURE OF VIOLENCE

Violence does not necessarily
take people by the throat and strangle them.
Usually it demands no more
than an oath of allegiance from its subjects.
They are required merely to become accomplices in its lies.

— *Aleksandr Solzhenitsyn*

YOUR CHILDREN

Your children will have to live with ours.

— *An Iraqi teacher before the war*

HEAR THE CRIES

God,
come now and hear the cries of those in need:
all who are defeated and discouraged by life itself,
the children who are hungry,
the homeless who have no place to sleep,
the women who are abused and battered,
the men who know only grief and regret,
the prisoners who are without friends,
the physically and mentally challenged who are neglected,
the unborn who cannot discover breath and life,
the executed who have no one to cry for them,

the elderly who are pushed away and forgotten,
the gay and lesbian who are judged, feared, and scorned,
the sick and the ill who are alone,
the believers of different sacred traditions who are misunderstood.

God, come now; hear our cries.

Amen.

— DH

LET JUSTICE ROLL

I hate and I despise your ceremonies,
and I take no delight in your solemn assemblies and gatherings.
Even though you offer me your offerings and sacrifices,
I will not accept them.
I am not impressed.
Take away from me the noise of your songs;
I will not listen to your melodies,
your playing, your strumming,
your drumming, or your singing.
Save me your songs!
But let justice roll down like a river
and righteousness like an ever-flowing stream.

— adapted from Amos 5:21–24 by DH

GOODNESS IS STRONGER THAN EVIL

Goodness is stronger than evil;
love is stronger than hate;
light is stronger than darkness;
life is stronger than death.
Victory is ours through him who loved us.

— Desmond Tutu

GREAT COMPASSION

When we begin to see that black mud and white snow
are neither ugly nor beautiful,
when we can see them without discrimination or duality,
then we begin to grasp Great Compassion.
In the eyes of Great Compassion,
there is neither left nor right, friend nor enemy, close or far.
Don't think that Great Compassion is lifeless.
The energy of Great Compassion is radiant and wondrous.
In the eyes of Great Compassion,
there is no separation between subject and object,
    no separate self.
Nothing can disturb Great Compassion.

— *Thich Nhat Hanh*

TEACH YOUR CHILDREN

Teach your children
what we have taught our children—
that the earth is our mother.
Whatever befalls the earth
befalls the children of the earth.
This we know.
The earth does not belong to us;
we belong to the earth.

— *Chief Seattle*

WE MUST CHOOSE

We must choose sides, not between nations,
but between the world's way and Christ's way.
The world hates; God loves.

— *Dorothy Day*

MEAL BLESSINGS

PRAYER BEFORE MEALS

Bless us, O Lord, and these your gifts,
which we are about to receive from your bounty,
through Christ, our Lord.

Amen.

BLESSED ARE YOU

Blessed are you, Lord our God,
Ruler of the universe,
for you bring forth bread from the earth.

— *ancient Jewish table blessing*

YOU BRING BREAD

You bring bread from the earth
and wine to gladden our hearts.

— *adapted from Psalm 104:14–15*

THE EYES OF ALL HOPE IN YOU

The eyes of all hope in you, O God,
and you give us food in due season.
You open your hand,
and every creature is filled with your blessings.

— *adapted from Psalm 104:27–28*

GOD, I THANK YOU

God,
I thank you for the blessings and gifts
that you have provided for me and my relatives
and the food that you have provided also.
I pray that we will receive strength
and good health from it.
So be it.

— *Lakota prayer*

JOINING HANDS

Everyone at table
joins hands for a silent moment.

— *Quaker prayer*

BLESSING OF THE MEAL

God of this meal and every meal,
we gather here at your table of grace.
We come with all of our hungers,
aching for you to strengthen us,
to fill us,
and to sustain us.
Help us to eat, drink,
and share this food with grace
and with gratitude and care.
May this food that we share
and our words and laughter
become a feast of love.
May your grace,
your love,
your life,
touch and embrace us.

Amen.

— *DH*

BEFORE YOU TASTE

Before you taste anything,
recite a blessing.

— *Rabbi Akiva*

ALL IS ONE

The ritual is One.
The food is One.
We who offer the food are One.
The fire of hunger is also One.
All action is One.
We who understand this are One.

— *Hindu food blessing*

THE BANQUET OF LOVE

We come to join in the banquet of love.
Let it open our hearts
and break down the fears
that keep us from loving each other.

— *The Dominican Sisters*

THANKSGIVING AFTER THE MEAL

We give you thanks for all your benefits
almighty God,
who lives and reigns forever and ever.

Amen.

MORE PRAYERS AND BLESSINGS

TAKE, O TAKE ME AS I AM

Take, O take me as I am;
summon out what I shall be;
set your seal upon my heart
and live in me.

— *John Bell*

TODAY, O LORD

Today, O Lord—I say YES to you!
Today, O Lord—I say YES to life!
Today, O Lord—I say YES to truth!
Today, O Lord—I say YES to kindness!
Today, O Lord—I say YES to gentleness!
Today, O Lord—I say YES to honesty!
Today, O Lord—I say YES to peace!
Today, O Lord—I say YES to compassion!
Today, O Lord—I say YES to community!
Today, O Lord—I say YES to goodness!
Today, O Lord—I say YES to beauty!
Today, O Lord—I say YES to joy!
Today, O Lord—I say YES to healing!
Today, O Lord—I say YES to love!

— *DH*

LET US TAKE CARE

Let us take care of the children,
for they have a long way to go.

Let us take care of the elders,
for they have come a long way.

Let us take care of those in between,
for they are doing the work.

— *African prayer*

HELP ME TO PRAY

God,
help me to feel free enough to let go,
to let you take over,
to accept your presence.

Transform my ego to give way to humble service.

Set free my self-consciousness,
lighten my worry and my need to control outcomes.

Accept my prayer;
help me to accept you.

Send me the gift of breath,
that I may greet with joy the spirit
that I know
is singing deep within my heart.

Amen.

— *DH*

A PRAYER

O our Father, the Sky,
hear us and make us strong.

O our Mother, the Earth,
hear us and give us support.

O Spirit of the East,
send us your Wisdom.

O Spirit of the South,
may we tread your path of life.

O Spirit of the West,
may we always be ready for the long journey.

O Spirit of the North, purify us
with your cleansing winds.

— *Sioux prayer*

OPEN UNTO ME

Open unto me—light for my darkness.
Open unto me—courage for my fear.
Open unto me—hope for my despair.
Open unto me—peace for my turmoil.
Open unto me—joy for my sorrow.
Open unto me—strength for my weakness.
Open unto me—wisdom for my confusion.
Open unto me—forgiveness for my sins.
Open unto me—tenderness for my toughness.
Open unto me—love for my hates.
Open unto me—Thy Self for my self,

Lord, Lord, open unto me!

Amen.

— *Howard Thurman*

GOD, I OFFER MYSELF TO YOU

God,
I offer myself to you—
to build with me
and do with me as you will.
Relieve me of the bondage of self,
that I may better do your will.
Take away my difficulties,
that victory over them may bear witness
to those I would help of your power,
your love,
and your way of life.
May I do your will always.

— *Alcoholics Anonymous*

WHAT IS YOUR NAME?

Who are you, God; where do you live?
High in the mountains,
deep in the ocean—are you the wind?

Are you the rain, or the roar of the sea?
Spinner of chaos,
breathing and stirring deep within?

Fire of love, healer of tears,
friend of the lonely,
bread for the hungry, hope for the poor!

Dancer of life, mystery of death;
giver and taker, loving creator,
guiding light!

You, our desire, maker of dreams;
voice of the trumpet,
author of silence, blossom of truth!

Wonder of strength, compassion, and calm,
singer of mercy, source of our safety,
justice and peace!

All of your ways are here in our midst:
presence and absence, laughter and anger;
life and death!

What is your name? How are you known?
Mother or father? Sister or brother?
You are God—beyond our words!

— DH

MAY THE ROAD RISE TO MEET YOU

May the road rise to meet you,
may the wind be at your back.
May the sun shine warm upon your face.
May the rain fall softly on your fields,
and until we meet again,
may you keep safe in the gentle, loving arms of God.

— an Irish blessing (adapted by Lori True)

THE GREAT MYSTERY

May the Great Mystery
make sunrise in your heart.

—Sioux blessing

SUFI BLESSING

May the blessing of God rest upon us.
May God's peace abide in us.
May God's presence illuminate our hearts,
now and forevermore.

— a Sufi blessing

MAY GOD BLESS YOU

May God bless you and keep you.
May God watch over you with kindness.
May God grant you a life of good health, joy, and peace.

— traditional Jewish blessing

MAY CHRIST GIVE TO YOU

May Christ give to you
at this time and for always—
his peace in your soul,
his presence in your heart,
his power in your life.

— *an Irish blessing*

SALAAM ALEIKUM

May peace be in your hearts.
May peace be in your homes.
May peace be in your land.
May peace be in our world.

— *a prayer from Ghana*

YOU HAVE BEEN ENLIGHTENED

You have been enlightened by Christ.
Walk always as children of the light
and keep the flame of faith alive in your hearts.

— *from the* Rite of Christian Initiation of Adults, Sacraments of Initiation

WALK IN THE LIGHT OF CHRIST

You have followed God's light
and the way of the Gospel now lies open to you.
Walk in the light of Christ,
and learn to trust in his wisdom.

— *from the* Rite of Christian Initiation of Adults, Rite of Acceptance

REFERENCES

In addition to the original prayers written by David Haas for this collection, every effort has been made to trace the sources for many of the other prayers in this book. If any sources have been omitted, it is unintentional. GIA Publications, Inc., will be pleased to rectify any omission in future editions.

The prayers "Good Morning," "A Prayer for the Evening," "A Night Prayer," "When I Am Anxious or Stressed," "When There Is Conflict," "When There Are Distractions," "For the Gift of Hospitality and Welcome," and "Help Me to Pray" are adapted from *With Every Note I Sing* by David Haas, copyright © 1995 GIA Publications, Inc., Chicago. (G-4392)

The prayers "Prayer for the Morning," "As the Evening Begins," and "Help Me to Let Go" are adapted from *I Will Sing Forever* by David Haas, copyright © 2000 GIA Publications, Inc., Chicago. (G-5649)

"Blest Are You / Gospel Canticle" text by David Haas is from *Walking by Faith* by David Haas and Robert Piercy, copyright © 1998 GIA Publications, Inc., Chicago. (G-4831FS)

"Blessing" for Morning and Evening Prayer, originally titled, "Final Blessing," by David Haas is from the collection *We Give You Thanks*, G-4989, and *Gather Comprehensive: Second Edition*, G-6200, copyright © 2005 GIA Publications, Inc., Chicago.

"Magnificat / All That I Am / Gospel Canticle" by David Haas, copyright © 1988 GIA Publications, Inc., Chicago. (G-3447)

"Beneath Thy Tender Care" by Dietrich Bonhoeffer is from *Letters and Papers from Prison*, edited by Eberhard Bethge, copyright © 1971 Macmillan, New York.

"Watch, O Lord" by Marty Haugen, copyright © 2003 GIA Publications, Inc., Chicago. (G-6310)

"The Name of God" by David Haas (also found in the collections *As Water to the Thirsty*, G-3062, and *Psalms for the Church Year, Vol. 3*, G-3325), copyright © 1987 GIA Publications, Inc., Chicago. (G-3498)

"Like a Little Child" by David Haas (also found in the collection *No Longer Strangers*, G-3946), copyright © 1993 GIA Publications, Inc., Chicago. (G-3956)

"Before I Was Born" by David Haas, copyright © 2000 GIA Publications, Inc., Chicago. (G-5182)

"Let Your Gentleness Be Known," originally titled "The Peace of God" by David Haas (also found in the collection *With You by My Side*, G-5785M, and on the recording *Reach Toward Heaven*, CD-566), copyright © 2002 GIA Publications, Inc., Chicago. (G-5817)

"Nada de Turbe," adapted by David Haas, is from the collection *God Is Here*, copyright © 2005 GIA Publications, Inc., Chicago. (G-6686)

"The Only Necessary Thing," "Our Desire for God," "Our Deepest Fear," "God's Initiative," and "Without Prayer" by Henri J. M. Nouwen are from *The Only Necessary Thing: Living a Prayerful Life*, edited by Wendy Wilson Greer, copyright © 1999 Crossroad Publishing Company, New York.

"Outside Your Comfort Zone," "The Purpose of Prayer," "The Great and Merciful Surprise," "Doing His Journey," "True Prayer," and "Our Own Center" by Richard Rohr are from *Everything Belongs: The Gift of Contemplative Prayer*, rev. ed., copyright © 1999, 2003 Richard Rohr. Crossroad Publishing Company, New York.

"Abide, O Spirit of Life" by William Huebsch is from the collection *God Is Here* (GIA Publications, Inc., Chicago) and copyright © 2005 by William Huebsch. (G-6686)

"Perfect Charity" by David Haas (also found in the collection *Glory Day*, G-4849), copyright © 1997 GIA Publications, Inc., Chicago. (G-4745)

"Jesus Needs Us" by Joseph Bernardin is from *The Gift of Peace: Personal Reflections,* copyright © 1997 Loyola Press, Chicago.

"Our Deepest Fear" by Marianne Williamson is from *A Return to Love: Reflections on the Principles of a Course in Miracles*, copyright © 1992 HarperCollins, New York.

"That I May See" by Pierre Teilhard de Chardin is from *Hymn of the Universe*, translated by Simon Bartholomew, copyright © 1965, Harper & Row, New York.

"The Long Loneliness" by Dorothy Day is from *The Long Loneliness: The Autobiography of Dorothy Day*, copyright © 1952 Harper, New York.

"Dare to Love" by Henri Nouwen is from *The Inner Voice of Love: A Journey through Anguish to Freedom*, copyright © 1996 Doubleday, New York.

"More than Ever" by Pedro Arrupe is from *One Jesuit's Spiritual Journey: Autobiographical Conversations with Jean-Claude Dietsch,* copyright © 1986 Institute of Jesuit Sources, St. Louis.

"Prayer for Peace" by David Haas (also found in the collections *As Water to the Thirsty,* G-3062, *Glory Day,* G-4849, and *Walking by Faith,* G-4831), copyright © 1987 GIA Publications, Inc., Chicago. (G-3505)

"Peace," "What Gospel?" and "Where God Is" by Oscar Romero are from *The Violence of Love: The Pastoral Wisdom of Archbishop Oscar Romero*, copyright © 1988, Harper & Row, San Francisco.

"In Spite of Everything" by Anne Frank is from *The Diary of a Young Girl,* translated from the Dutch by B. M. Mooijaart-Doubleday, introduction by Eleanor Roosevelt, copyright © 1952 Doubleday, Garden City, New York.

"Take, O Take Me As I Am" by John Bell is from *Two Songs of Commitment,* © 1995 GIA Publications, Inc., Chicago. (G-5285)

"What Is Your Name?" by David Haas (also found in the collection *I Shall See God*, G-3386), copyright © 1990 GIA Publications, Inc., Chicago. (G-3452)

"May the Road Rise to Meet You" by Lori True (also found in the collection *A Place at the Table,* G-6061), copyright © 2003 GIA Publications, Inc., Chicago. (G-6066)

"You Have Been Enlightened" and "Walk in the Light of Christ" are from *The Rite of Christian Initiation of Adults*, Bishops' Committee on the Liturgy, study edition, copyright © 1988, United States Conference of Catholic Bishops, Washington, DC.

ABOUT THE AUTHOR

David Haas is director of The Emmaus Center for Music, Prayer, and Ministry and serves as campus minister / artist-in-residence at Benilde-St. Margaret's High School in St. Louis Park, Minnesota. Well known as one of the preeminent liturgical composers in the English-speaking world, he has recorded more than forty-five collections of original liturgical music and has written more than twenty books on the topics of music, liturgy, religious education, youth ministry, prayer, and spirituality. He has traveled throughout the United States, Canada, the British Isles, Ireland, Europe, Australia, Israel, Greece, and Turkey as a conference and workshop speaker, concert performer, retreat leader, and recording artist and was nominated for a Grammy Award in 1991 for the recording *I Shall See God* (GIA Publications, Inc.). He is a regular columnist for *Ministry and Liturgy* magazine and the founder and director of Music Ministry Alive!, a national liturgical music formation program for high school and college-aged youth.